From Mii Li Wit Love

Mii Li Fortner

BookLeaf Publishing

India | USA | UK

Made with ❤ on the BookLeaf Publishing Platform

www.bookleafpub.in

www.bookleafpub.com

Dedication

To da community that supports and loves me for me.
To my chosen family who are always there.

Preface

Always enjoyed communicating through words.
These are poems from a small but crucial time period in
my life journey.

Acknowledgements

To muses past present and future, life is a journey to be enjoyed 😁

4. Why

Why
So many reason why
Maybe not sports ball but musically inclined
Not great at chess but wanting to get to know me so
deep to get meaningful gifts
Why
Have not learned to change oil but gives your heart
treating others like royals
Say not a handy person yet able to build sets
Why
Same space when it is not just about sex
Why
Self reliant commanding persons who are defiant
Why
Fashion shows, great talks, long walks, being silly, just
there chilling with me
Why
Your warmth, your beauty, willingness to try
A bad ass playlist that makes me cry
Why
Because who you are...if writing a review 5 out of 5 stars
:)
Why
After one date...songs, words, thingies make me

appreciate and linger

Why

A person who would trust if I asked to pull my finger,
hahaha

5. Can't Sleep

Thunder wakes me from my bed
I gave a startled cry
Lighting sprawled through darkened clouds
I only wonder tonight

My heart did flutter ever more
At sight of your reply
Then when so rudely waken
From storms and roaring skys

I wonder what spells you possess
To make me shutter so
For now all I can do is guess
For I may never know

7. In Your Garden

We walked the gardens hand in hand
Surrounded by the scent
of tropical plumerias
We looked in wonderment

The many flowers fluttered round
A rainbow at a glace
I cannot cease my pondering
over meeting happenstance

We wandered among many trees
Their branches covered and bent
Flowers fallen across the paths
Their fleeting beauty spent

All the colors, all the blooms
with such variety
There are so many ways to love
We are learning to see

9. China Town

So many ways to love, yet one so familiar to me
So many tastes delicious on thy tongue
So many plates so many of da funs
So many firsts have come from dis night

Linens fresh from grass stained elixir
Smokey tire fire lay on lips to only kiss but her
Green hearts did tame da beast
Already weakened with godly feasts of cured meats

Share drink and dine to and fro
Yet pirates call with yet 2 minutes to go

A chariot Yet awaits on a street corner high from da date

Cards before da night expires
Whom raises da bar of what's desired

Day breaks as we lay in bed
A heat source found while hands on warm skin are lead

Drink sweet bean before you bid fairwell
One more embrace one more time neck to smell

11. First Kiss

6

So timid since day one when you sat close on your couch
Stare at your lips they say words without speaking
Long embraces ending with warm eyes
I miss you before we even say goodbye
Crave everything about you
Had my dreams come true
Soon to meet again
Let lips touch softly

19. Burning Time

Meet you at a rave, already eyes...behave
A pirate at my heart eager to speak
Walk you home why do I feel so...at home
Date one growing connections over art
Is this a date we said...and It starts
Not wanting time with you to end
Lets plan another date... you picked heels
I hear you date 2 was a surprise reveal
Hands touch for the first time while fireworks go in da mind
First cuddle...first time bodies feel warmth
Get a whole day wit you on date 3
Conversing over long walks through rainbows and trees
My hands around your waist for an embrace
Your hands pull me closer
Rain misses us like some one is watching
Car chaos you support...somehow not spoiling da mood
We get ready for a night of fun, laughs, elixir and food
Sharing all da kine we went to every place together
Happenstance you say...I say so lovely to meet her
More cuddles...now first time in bed
So much warmth so many thingies in my head
Today is date 1.5 my head already over my heels
________ you give me all...of da feels!

12. Still Awake

Waking next to you
Your nightmares continue but no bother Mii Li is here
Cuddling, kissing, holding, nibbling on your ear
Endless curves as you take your beauty rest
A warmth in your hand as it runs over my breast
Your eyes see, see my love but hold so much beneath
Massage your back as we caress
Flip over now I am on top "a great view" you said
Can't get enough of your kiss
My lips, my neck, my hand, my body
In elevators as I get naughty
You hold my hand and I see your smile I see your lips
I see your eyes and to my suprise
I see a life side by side

13. Girl Friends not

Your memories plastered on pages songs of the ages
Electricity from brain to heart enough to start a fire
Heart on sleeve no longer in cages
So many thoughts of us two intertwined, from a gentle
peck
To a deep long caress
We talk about all da kine getting to know each other
Past slowly fade behind
We are not really strangers levels 1, 2 and 3
Who knew self love would be so spicy
Share a hand, a chocolate, drinks, a bed,
a kiss, a kitchen, a dance...what did I miss
Your are worth the wait, let me be the first to ask you
out on a date
Find yourself as do I, grow together into something
devine
I will be here gladly waiting for our 1 or 2 days
Glady dance da night away until we are old and gray
Until then continue to feast on fresh memories
Lets hang out whateva we may be
continue enjoying each others company

14. Holigays

As holidays begin and you start to slowly meet my
friends
I introduced you as a friend
The day is complete with you
Holidays were always so heavy so lonely so sad
Already want to schedule the next event
the next time to have peps meet you
Time flies yet is so still when next to you
My heart beats first than skips a beat when your near me
Just found out electricity and tangles and chills with
your touch and nibble
Not dat you need it but friends approve
Friends protect Mii Li's heart...has been beaten and
bruised
Not knowing what was looking for
Seems to have found

15. 3rd Base

12

We cuddle, you enjoy my dress
See our hair a lioness
I can't stop looking at you
We kiss
Energies surge as we have to shake em out
always a new spot to explore
amazingly intense
I shy
Than we look again in each others eyes
My dress slides to da side
Your hand on my ass and thigh
 I kiss you on your neck and arm
A touch over a wet spot
Nervous I make a silly comment
You would be my first
Already have my heart
Emotions building fast
O how I hope and dream the moment will last

18. Not in Cursive

13

It is true I asked wrong questions about hands
All the while not knowing the power you have through a
pen
Am I blind to see thy lips when not speaking
Dang ol tongue talking when should have basked in da
joy of silence
Do not ask why, hand compose what hands compose
Hearts know only what hearts know
Future, not bitter past tents
A way forward is what is next
Buds need but few things to grow
Able to take any shape when growing slow

16. Dance Night

We warm up and I can do dis fu eva
Near you caught in da moment try saying something cleaver
Lost in ocean eyes peeks at slit over sexy thighs
We embrace so close can I sneak a kiss
We dance so fast n so slow never wanting to let go
You look so beautiful tonight like every night
My heart wrapped in warmth ooh such a delight
Notice my tigers, you pull out a chair, hold my hand
Gentle touches, bright lips on mind no words can describe
We talk about messing up hair and I am so there
We talk and I just want moments like these fo eva
You try with what mentals yo have to spare
I notice, so happy to be here
One month has it been
If this was sports ball, I feel I got da "big" win!
Three words can only discribe
Until den continue enjoying life side by side at dis time

17. Mess up Hair

15

Thoughts rush as start to cuddle
Take it to da bed as we continue
I kiss your lips...you I am soo into
Nibbling one's neck minds muddle
Temperature rises as bodies explored
Can't mess up hair...continue I want more and more
Let's touch skin...breast to breast
Can't lay down for hair would mess
Tongue adventures across a new land
Moans and bodies quiver
Multiple sweet spots deliver

3. Twas a Moment

16

Drawn towards you before our first date
Fell for you...can another relate?
Time flies when together
Frozen in time when alone
Sucka for romance we kiss on the middle of a bridge
You're all I see when your near me
Want to dance with you anywhere
On top of a pillbox to Eton Square
You're all I think about...your my muse
From screams of happyness
To karaoke da blues
Do you think of me the way I think of you

10. Time Travels

17

Time drags on as chores dwindle down
Another chapter closed as anew found
Storms have passed leaving wake
Adding to it slightly to da ever growing plate
Happy times wit da Kiddos
Queerness breakng da mold
Soon to take flight over land and seas
Hopping you'll be the first sight I see

1. New Friend

"We were looking for the same thing"
     you replied
An answer dat caught me by suprise
My favorite photo is of you
That smile I would like to make
That laugh I could relate
Those eyes I should not stare
Wanting to learn what is behind
What thoughts run freely in your mind
"I was ready"
     for dat same question
We both seemed to like each others answers
Can there be more phone calls, movie nights
Dancing and proms, more unplanned hangouts
More time getting to know you
More time would be...pretty cool
Life long friend

6. Strangers

Light shines through clouds as darkness looms
Two strangers meet under a crimson moon
Eyes glance and repeat
Courage to talk small about nothing
Yet bodies say it all
What an amazing aura
Those who don't understand jump away
Deep connections bask and stay
Shall we dance, feet say
Shall we hug, arms say
Shall we kiss, lips insist
Shall we leap...hearts no regrets
Shall we see each other, eyes agree
No longer strangers
This night we did by happenstance
Unexpectedly we did meet

8. Future You

Eyes meet, I blush and stare at feet
You smile and ask to stay awhile
We talk for hours
Connection building buds into flowers
I make you laugh
Seamless and deep convo did we attract
Authentically ones self we did interact
Ended the day not wanting to leave
A long hug gentle eyes gaze at thy
Until next time we meet
Next time I will not look at your feet

2. Future Me

Fall into those eyes, let them be kind
Let her be a stranger or a friend
Be in the present no worries of pasts or ends
Don't be shy and many first you should try
Even if it hurts neva lie
Love her like you want to be loved
You have so much to give don't settle
Think with clear mind don't act when muddled
She will see you and understand what she sees
Threat her like you want to be treated
Your hearts full to give no matter how much once it
bleeded
Cry your eyes out, in joy, in peace, in love and war
Feel emotions like on da dance floor
Listen to her like music
Just be you and that's your truth
For the right time she will fall for you
Love yourself that's what you can do